CENTER STAGE

SYLVESTER STALLONE

By
William Sanford
Carl Green

Edited By
Dr. Howard Schroeder
Professor in Reading and Language Arts
Dept. of Elementary Education
Mankato State University

Produced & Designed By
Baker Street Productions, Ltd.

CRESTWOOD HOUSE

Mankato, Minnesota
U.S.A.

JB
STALLONE
(Sylvester)
Sanford

LIBRARY OF CONGRESS CATALOGING IN PUBLICATION DATA

Sanford, William R. (William Reynolds), 1927-
   Sylvester Stallone

   (Center stage)
   Bibliography: p.
   1. Stallone, Sylvester—Juvenile literature. 2. Moving-picture actors and actresses—United States—Biography—Juvenile Literature. I. Green, Carl R. II. Schroeder, Howard.
III. Title. IV. Series.
PN2287.S667S36   1986   791.43'028'0924 [B]   86-8898
ISBN 0-89686-304-2

International Standard   Library of Congress
Book Number: Catalog Card Number:
0-89686-304-2   86-8898

ILLUSTRATION CREDITS:

Wide World Photo: Cover, 6, 13, 14, 17, 18, 21, 23, 24, 27, 28
Scott R. Alonzo/LGI: 5
People in Pictures/LGI: 10
UPI/Bettmann Newsphotos: 30

11/88 Crestwood 10.00

CRESTWOOD HOUSE

Hwy. 66 South, Box 3427
Mankato, MN 56002-3427
507-388-1616

83629

TABLE
OF
CONTENTS

INTRODUCTION

"The twelve million dollar superstar"

Who's the best movie star in Hollywood? Some people would name Dustin Hoffman or Robert Redford. Others might vote for Meryl Streep or Sally Field. Who can really judge? All four have made many popular movies.

There's one certain way of judging actors, however. Moviemakers pay the biggest salaries to the biggest stars. By that yardstick, there's no contest. As of 1986, Sylvester Stallone was the big winner. After the success of *Rocky IV*, Stallone was asking $12 million (US) a picture—and getting it! That's twice as much as Redford's $6 million (US) per movie.

Is anyone worth that much money? Babe Ruth, the greatest of all baseball players, answered that question. Back in 1930, Ruth was demanding a big new contract. Newspaper reporters teased him about it. One of them asked, "What makes you think you should earn more than the President of the United States?" Babe Ruth shot back, "I had a better year than he did!"

Sylvester Stallone has earned his place at the top.

Sylvester Stallone earned his way to the top.

Stallone has starred in some of the top money-making movies of all time. Ever since his 1976 success with *Rocky*, "Sly" Stallone has been a "bankable." That's what movie producers call someone whose movies are sure to sell lots of tickets.

How good is Stallone at selling tickets? Ask the producers of *Rambo: First Blood Part II*. Movie fans packed the theaters to see the movie when it opened in June of 1985. By the end of the year, the film had taken in over $200 million (US). That's not bad for a movie that cost only $27 million (US) to make!

Rambo was a movie hit!

CHAPTER ONE

Growing up wasn't easy

Stallone started out in life as a thin, unhappy boy who was always in trouble. But Stallone has a lot of Rocky Balboa (his movie character) in him. Like Rocky, he fought his way to the top. Stallone even gave the boxer a special nickname: "the Italian Stallion." The reason isn't hard to find. Stallone means "stallion" in Italian.

Michael Sylvester Stallone was born in New York City on June 6, 1946. The Stallone family lived in the tough Hell's Kitchen area of Manhattan. The boy's father was an Italian named Frank Stallone. Frank was studying to be a hairdresser. His mother, Jacqueline, worked as a dancer to help pay the bills.

The doctor pinched a nerve on the left side of Sylvester's face during his birth. The injury made his left eye and the left side of his mouth turn down. Later on, the injury also made it hard for him to speak clearly. As a child, his looks made the other kids laugh at him. As an actor, Sylvester Stallone has overcome his handicaps.

A "hyper" little kid

Both of the Stallone parents worked hard. There wasn't anyone at home to take care of Sylvester. The baby spent Monday through Friday at a foster home. Stallone remembers himself as a "hyper" little kid. He was always getting into trouble. When he was only three years old, for example, Sylvester painted some cars with red paint. Frank Stallone spanked his son hard and often, but with little effect. Sylvester kept getting into trouble.

A second child, Frank, Jr., was born in 1950. Like most brothers, Sylvester and Frank fought and argued. But they always loved each other. The Stallones didn't want their sons growing up in Hell's Kitchen. They moved to Silver Springs, Maryland. Frank Stallone opened his own beauty shop.

Sylvester doesn't have many happy memories of this time. When he went to school, the other kids teased him because of the injury to his face. His name was a problem, too. Even today, he remembers being called "Sylvester Puddytat." When things got too bad, Sylvester fought back. He had at least one fight a month. The lonely boy often imagined himself as a hero named "Sly." Today, his friends still call him by that name.

In 1957, Frank and Jacqueline broke up. Constant arguments finally led to a divorce. From then on, Sylvester lived with his mother one year and his father the next. His mother moved to Philadelphia and remarried. There she opened a gym where women could work out.

A creative trouble maker

By that time, Sylvester had been thrown out of a dozen schools. His sense of humor often got him into trouble. For example, he once wrote a paper about what it felt like to eat a car. The teacher wasn't amused. Later, at a Catholic school, he ate the puddings meant for the nuns. Finally, his mother put him in a school for students with special problems. Sylvester liked the school and began to settle down.

When he was thirteen, Sylvester began lifting weights. His thin arms and chest became hard and muscular. More sure of himself, he didn't worry so much about making people like him. He made some friends and began to play sports. Sylvester's grades were still poor, however. Lifting weights and talking to girls didn't leave much time for study.

Frank Stallone told his son, "You weren't born with much of a brain, so you'd **better** develop your body." Sylvester never forgot those unkind words. He gave the same line to Rocky Balboa in the first *Rocky* movie. But Sylvester did have a good brain. He went to an American college in Switzerland. There he learned to read good books, to study art, and to enjoy writing.

Stallone loves to act.

Acting turns him on

College also gave Sylvester a chance to act. Making a part come to life made him feel good about himself. He could be whomever he wanted to be—and people would clap for him. Sylvester's new interest in acting led him to the University of Miami in 1969. However, the drama teachers at Miami told him he'd never be an actor. As usual, Sylvester didn't give up. He started his own acting group. The actors put on plays wherever they could find a stage.

The audiences liked Sylvester's work. But Miami wasn't the big time. Sylvester quit school and headed for New York. He was sure he could make it on the Broadway stage.

CHAPTER TWO

Making it as an actor and writer

Sylvester Stallone didn't set New York on fire. Acting jobs were hard to find. He worked at odd jobs to keep himself going. One of his jobs was sweeping out the lion cages at a zoo. Sylvester admired the hardworking people he saw every day. He promised that someday he would create heroes these people could cheer.

Jacqueline Stallone read her son's star chart. She told him his first success would be as a writer. Sylvester bought a book on scriptwriting. He wrote every night after a hard day's work. Sometimes he was so tired he fell asleep at his desk.

Sasha helps out

In 1970, Sylvester met Sasha Czach. They were working at the same theater. The beautiful Sasha couldn't resist Sylvester's charm. He even cut his long hair to please her. Sasha gave up her own plans to become an actress. She worked as a waitress so Sylvester could go on acting and writing. One day, Sylvester was able to write six thirty-minute television scripts. One of them sold for $2,500 (US). But he still couldn't make a big sale.

Sylvester didn't give up on his acting, either. He practiced in front of a mirror each day. Then he went to auditions. An audition is a tryout where directors pick the actors they need for a play or film. In 1971, Sylvester won a small part in a Woody Allen film called *Bananas*. He also appeared in a few plays.

Finally, a good part in *The Lords of Flatbush* came his way. *Time* magazine said that Stallone's work was one of the best parts in the film. Henry Winkler was also in the film. Winkler later copied Stallone's character when he created The Fonz on television's *Happy Days*.

Hollywood, watch out!

Stallone next decided to try his luck in Hollywood. He put Sasha and their dog into a forty-dollar car and drove to California. An agent tried to help him, but Sylvester didn't find much work. A few bit parts in television shows kept him going. Many other young actors would have given up. But Sylvester kept trying. He got up every morning at 6:30 and worked on his scripts.

Finally, Sylvester's luck began to change. He sold his *Hell's Kitchen* script for $21,500 (US). Next, the movie parts started coming in. Sylvester played muggers and gangsters. He acted in *Farewell My Lovely* with Robert Mitchum and in *Capone* with Ben Gazzara. Those roles won him a better part in *Death Race 2000*. Sylvester played a nasty race car driver who gets blown up at the end of the film. Then he got some bad news. Paramount Pictures decided not to film *Hell's Kitchen*.

Rocky is born

By March of 1975, Sylvester and Sasha were almost broke again. Still searching for a perfect idea, Sylvester went to a boxing match. Underdog Chuck Wepner surprised everyone by putting up a good fight against Champion Muhammad Ali. Sylvester felt inspired. He created Rocky Balboa that same night.

The character of Rocky Balboa was inspired by a real boxing match.

Rocky was a big hit.

Rocky is a good fighter, Sylvester decided, but he doesn't get the breaks. He makes his living by collecting money for a loan shark. Then he gets lucky. Almost as a joke, the champion offers Rocky a title fight. In Sylvester's first script, Rocky loses the big fight. Two producers read the script and told Sylvester that they liked the story. "Now, give us a happy ending," they said.

Sylvester raced home to work on a second draft. Sasha typed while he talked. They kept going for eighty-six hours. In the new script, Rocky loses the fight, but wins everyone's respect.

United Artists offered to buy *Rocky* for $75,000 (US). There was one catch. The studio wanted a big-name actor to play Rocky. Sylvester said he wouldn't sell the script unless he played Rocky. He had only $106 (US) in the bank, but he would not change his mind. The offers to buy the script got larger, but Sylvester said "no" to each one. United Artists finally gave in. Sylvester Stallone had won the part of a lifetime.

14

CHAPTER THREE

Rocky wins an Oscar

As he began work on *Rocky*, Sylvester was starting a rags-to-riches movie career. *Rocky* and *Rambo* would make him a superstar. But some of his other movies would fail at the box office.

That was all in the future when United Artists agreed to make *Rocky*. The studio didn't want to take any chances. It put up only $1 million (US) to make the film. UA also worried that Sylvester was too small to play Rocky Balboa. The actor argued that his seventeen-inch (43 cm) biceps were bigger than those of many heavyweight champions. Aside from his small size, Sylvester really did look like a heavyweight boxer. At 5'10'' (178 cm) and 175 pounds (80 kg), he was in great shape.

Sylvester trained as if he was going to fight a real champion. For five months, he got up at dawn and ran on the beach. Then he went to the gym to work on his boxing. As Rocky, Sylvester had to fight flat-footed. His style was to move in, taking three blows to get in one of his own. He told the fighters he boxed with not to hold back on their punches. They didn't. Sylvester learned what it felt like to get knocked down.

Rocky was filmed in four weeks in Sylvester's old home town of Philadelphia. The film crew made good use of the city's streets, run-down gyms, and old apartments. The whole Stallone family got into the act. Brother Frank sang, and Sylvester's father played a small part. Sasha took still photos of the filming. Even the Stallone's dog had a part.

The film opened in November of 1976. It was a big hit right from the start. The fans loved Stallone and Talia Shire, who played Rocky's girlfriend. But most of all, they cheered Rocky's "go for it" courage. Rex Reed, a film critic, summed up their feelings this way: "...*Rocky* [is] likeable and decent in a basic way that makes the heart glow."

Rocky won three Oscars, including best film of the year. Sylvester wasn't upset when he didn't win as best actor. He made $2 million (US) from *Rocky*. Better yet, producers now wanted him for other films. At the same time, people kept asking him if he was going to make a second *Rocky*. Sylvester said "no." Later events, however, changed his mind.

The Rockys add up

Sylvester's two 1978 films didn't match *Rocky's* success. But Rocky Balboa was still a winner. So Syl-

A belt patterned after the heavyweight championship belt was given to Stallone after Rocky became famous.

vester turned back to the Italian Stallion in 1979. In *Rocky II*, Sylvester let Rocky get married. Rocky promises his wife he will give up boxing. But then he runs out of money. He has to agree to a rematch with Apollo Creed. This time, Rocky wins and becomes champion. The film was another huge success.

With that track record, a third *Rocky* was sure to follow. Sylvester was paid $10 million (US) in 1982, for *Rocky III*. He was writer, director, and star. This time, Rocky faces Clubber Lang (played by Mr. T.) Clubber beats Rocky in their first fight. But Rocky won't quit. They fight again, and Rocky regains his title.

For *Rocky III*, Sylvester worked out harder than ever. He trimmed down to less than five percent body fat (the average man has twenty percent). The workouts gave Sylvester a forty-seven-inch (120 cm) chest and a thirty-inch (76 cm) waist. He also speeded up the action. The final round in the first *Rocky* had thirty-five blows. In *Rocky III*, the boxers threw 130 punches!

Rocky IV hit the theaters in 1985. This time, Rocky goes to Moscow to fight. The boxing match turns into a contest between America and Russia. Somehow, the aging Rocky comes back to knock out the "unbeatable" Russian boxer. Then he wraps the American flag around his shoulders. The critics hated the film, but audiences loved it.

Will there be another *Rocky*? No one knows for sure. As long as Rocky Balboa sells tickets, *Rocky V* can't be counted out. That's not enough for Sylvester, however. He wants to be known as more than a tough-guy star.

Rocky goes to Moscow, in Rocky IV, *to win a big fight.*

CHAPTER FOUR

The Stallone magic doesn't always work

Rocky made Sylvester Stallone a rich man. Sylvester moved into a big house and drove his new Mercedes to the studio everyday. He worked hard on a number of new films. But none of them measured up to Rocky, or to the Rambo films still to come.

In 1978's *F.I.S.T.*, Sylvester played a labor leader. Like Rocky, Johnny Kovak is a tough guy with a good heart. Sylvester had to age twenty years during the film. He also had to make some powerful speeches— something Rocky would never do. Even so, Sylvester thought he did a good job in *F.I.S.T.* The public thought otherwise. The picture barely made back its $9 million (US) cost.

People began saying that Sylvester was a "one-hit star." Theater owners, however, said he sold more tickets than anyone else. With that in mind, Universal Studios tried a new way of selling Sylvester's next movie. The studio first printed his novel, *Paradise*

Alley. The book was about three brothers who try to escape the poverty of Hell's Kitchen. The studio hoped that the book would make people want to see the movie. The plan didn't work. The critics didn't like the novel, and the public didn't buy it.

Sylvester was worried, but he went ahead with the movie. This time, he was the director, writer, and star. He filmed *Paradise Alley* in New York, near where he lived as a small child. As Cosmo, Sylvester tries to turn his younger brother into a big-time wrestler. Cosmo is no Rocky, however. The movie didn't win the hearts of Stallone's fans. Luckily, Sylvester already had the contract for *Rocky II* in his pocket.

From cop to cabbie

The success of *Rocky II* in 1979, gave Sylvester a chance to try again. In a 1981 film called *Nighthawks*, he played a big city cop. Unlike Rocky, Sgt. Deke DaSilva is college educated. He talks a lot, and Sylvester's fans didn't like him.

Then came *Victory*, a World War II film about prisoners of war. Sylvester and the other prisoners play a violent game of soccer with a German team. Michael Caine was also in the film and the great John Huston directed. But *Victory* made even less money than *Paradise Alley*.

20

Rocky III and *First Blood* came out in 1982, and Sylvester was hot again. He liked the idea of doing a musical, so he teamed up with Dolly Parton in *Rhinestone*. Sylvester played a New York city cabdriver. To win a bet, Dolly tries to turn the cabbie into a country singer. The 1984 film was a flop, but it did make one thing clear—Frank is the singer in the family, not Sylvester!

By now the critics were tearing Sylvester apart. He could play Rocky, but could he do anything else? Sylvester wasn't beaten, however. Rambo was still around to rescue him.

Rambo II *was another movie hit for Stallone.*

CHAPTER FIVE

Rambo leads Stallone back to the top

By 1982, Sylvester had made three *Rocky* movies. Some critics looked at *Nighthawk* and *Victory* and said that Rocky was the only part he could play. The Stallone luck hadn't run out, however. In 1982, Sylvester made his first Rambo film.

John Rambo was the hero of a 1972 novel called *Blood Knot*. Warner Brothers bought the movie rights, but never got around to making the movie. Finally, two producers bought the script. They offered Sylvester $3.5 million (US) to play Rambo. He accepted, but demanded that Rambo be made ''more human.''

A human fighting machine

The script was rewritten. In the new version, John Rambo is a veteran who fought in Vietnam. He is also

Rambo is a veteran who fought in Vietnam.

a human fighting machine. The action starts when Rambo wanders into a small town. The police arrest him and try to give him a shave. Rambo goes wild. The razor triggers memories of being tortured in Vietnam.

The movie becomes a fight for survival. Rambo is not a cold-blooded killer, however. He tries to wound his enemies instead of killing them. During the chase scenes, Rambo survives falls, explosions, and a helicopter attack. Later on, he crashes a truck into a gas station and shoots up a police station.

. Rambo died in the film's first ending. The producers didn't like the death scene. They called Sylvester back

Stallone's acting provided audiences with a hero.

and shot a second ending. This time, Rambo was sent
to prison. That way, he would still be alive to make
another film.

Filming *First Blood* was hard on the actors. To make
one scene, Sylvester had to jump down into a tree. He
hit the tree so hard he broke four ribs. Later on,
Sylvester also burned his hand and hurt his back. After
his trips to the hospital, he went right back to work.

Rambo goes to Vietnam

The success of the first Rambo film led to *Rambo: First Blood Part II*. The action in this 1985 film was almost nonstop. Sylvester had to run, fight, climb, swim, and dive. He even had to learn to use a bow that shoots exploding arrows. As always, Sylvester worked overtime to make sure everything was done right.

This time out, Rambo finds some Americans in a hidden Vietnamese prison camp. He is ready to rescue them, but his own officers double-cross him. The government doesn't want the public to know that there are Americans alive in Vietnam. Rambo is captured and tortured. He escapes and begins a one-man war against the communists.

Rambo II made even more money than *First Blood*. Critics said there was too much killing, but Sylvester disagreed. He said that war is a bloody business, and he wanted his films to look real. The critics did agree on one thing. The film helped people forget the bad memories of the U.S. defeat in Vietnam. Cheering for Rambo's victory made audiences feel better about being Americans.

CHAPTER SIX

Years of success and change

Sylvester Stallone has come a long way from Hell's Kitchen. His new house sits high above the ocean in Pacific Palisades, California. A brick wall keeps people away from the house. Inside, Sylvester has hung paintings by famous artists on the walls. But Sasha doesn't live there with him.

Sylvester and Sasha were often unhappy despite their love for their two sons. Sage Moonblood Stallone was born in 1976, and Seargeoh (sounds like Sergio) was born in 1979. Sage is strong and healthy, but Seargeoh was born with a problem called autism. Seth, as he is known, often withdraws into his own private world. The Stallones do what they can for him, but no one knows how to cure autism.

The Stallones' marriage finally ended in 1985. Sylvester always seemed to be in and out of love with other women. Sasha moved out to make a new life for herself. A few months after the divorce, Sylvester married a beautiful Danish actress.

Brigitte Nielsen became Stallone's wife in 1985.

Family life and the price of fame

Sylvester met Brigitte Nielsen in December, 1984. The six-foot (1.83 m) actress and model was twenty-one years old. She had been in love with Sylvester since she saw *Rocky* in 1976. When she first came to live in New York City, she wrote to Sylvester. He didn't answer her letters. Finally, Sylvester came to New York on business. Brigitte found out where he was staying and sent him some of her pictures. Sylvester took one look at the photos and decided to meet Brigitte. When

Sylvester and Brigitte were photographed at the White House in Washington, D.C., at a 1985 party.

Brigitte opened the door, it was love at first sight—just like in the movies.

Despite the divorce and remarriage, Sylvester keeps in close touch with his sons. Sage is a lot like his father. He works out and is very strong. When he was nine, he could do over three hundred pushups. Sylvester doesn't want Sage to be another Rocky, however. He tells the boy to develop his brains, too. To help Seth, Sylvester raises money to aid in finding a cure for autism.

Fame and money create their own problems. Sylvester is a target for some weird people. Strangers call him on the telephone and threaten to hurt him. Sylvester knows that's because people think he **is** Rocky or Rambo. When he goes out, he takes a bodyguard with him. He also keeps guards on duty at his home.

What's next?

Sylvester never stops working. In Hollywood you're only as good as your last film. One of his new scripts is called *Cobra*. It's about a man who hunts down criminals who have escaped from the police. Sylvester is quick to tell people not to get the film mixed up with real life. It's the job of the police and the courts to punish those who break the law.

Will he make *Rocky V*? Sylvester says he isn't sure. What is certain is that he won't slow down. He explains

Stallone and John Travolta (right) attend the premiere of Staying Alive, a movie directed by Stallone.

his feelings this way: "I always feel I'm being chased by Father Time. I...want to accomplish as much as I can before the final gong sounds."

Sylvester Stallone's fans don't really care whether he makes *Rocky V, Rambo III,* or *Cobra I.* They just want to see their favorite actor beat up the bad guys one more time. When the next Stallone film opens, they'll be standing in line to buy tickets.

THE FILMS OF SYLVESTER STALLONE

Bananas, 1971
The Lords of Flatbush, 1974
Farewell My Lovely, 1975
Capone, 1975
Death Race 2000, 1975
Rocky, 1976
F.I.S.T., 1978
Paradise Alley, 1978
Rocky II, 1979
Nighthawks, 1981
Victory, 1981
Rocky III, 1982
First Blood, 1982
Rhinestone, 1984
Rambo: First Blood Part II, 1985
Rocky IV, 1985